# Heart, Blood, Heartbeat, Arrhythmia, Blood Pressure & Drug
## 心, 血, 心跳, 心律失常, 血壓和藥

*********************************************

### Stroke  (suffer paralysis) 中風

Bone, shoulder damaged

Hong Son Cheung
張洪聲

美商EHGBooks微出版公司
www.EHGBooks.com

EHG Books 公司出版
Amazon.com 總經銷
2020 年版權美國登記
未經授權不許翻印全文或部分
及翻譯為其他語言或文字
2020 年 EHGBooks 第一版

Copyright © 2020 by Hong Son Cheung
Manufactured in United States
Permission required for reproduction,
or translation in whole or part.
Contact：info@EHGBooks.com

ISBN-13：978-1-64784-010-5

# Contents

**Preface** .................................................................................................... 7

    In our Body ........................................................................................ 7

**Acknowledgement** ............................................................................... 9

**Chapter 1** ............................................................................................ 11

    Pressure in our human body .......................................................... 11

**Chapter 2** ............................................................................................ 13

    Heart *** Blood ............................................................................... 13

**Chapter 3** ............................................................................................ 15

    Flexible situation *** blood moving ............................................. 15

**Chapter 4** ............................................................................................ 17

    Arrhythmia ...................................................................................... 17

**Chapter 5** ............................................................................................ 21

    Drug Talk ........................................................................................ 21

**Chapter 6** ............................................................................................ 23

    Blood pressure ................................................................................ 23

**Chapter 7** ............................................................................................ 27

    Medicine .......................................................................................... 27

**Chapter 8** ............................................................................................ 38

    Blood Pressure value results ......................................................... 38

心，血，心跳，心律失常，血壓和藥（國際英文版）
中風（癱瘓），骨頭，肩膀疼痛

## Chapter 9 .................................................................................. 43
### My stroke Paralysis ........................................................................ 43
## Chapter 10 ................................................................................ 47
### Xarelto pill and condition ................................................................ 47
## Conclusion ............................................................................... 51

*Heart, Blood, Heartbeat, Arrhythmia, Blood Pressure & Drug*
*Stroke (suffer paralysis), Bone, Shoulder Damaged*

*To my Dearest mother,*

*Mm. Lee Tsing Chin*

*To remember her for imparting her culture education in our life*

謹將此書

獻給我最敬愛的母親

李劍青太夫人

以永誌她的教誨

心，血，心跳，心律失常，血壓和藥（國際英文版）
中風（癱瘓），骨頭，肩膀疼痛

*Also to my dearest father*

*Cheung Mo Liang*

*Heart, Blood, Heartbeat, Arrhythmia, Blood Pressure & Drug*
*Stroke (suffer paralysis), Bone, Shoulder Damaged*

To my dearest brother

Mr. Christopher Cheung Hing Hung

给我最愛的二哥

張洪弘先生

銘記感謝他對我們的家庭

這一生的種種照顧

To thank him for supporting all family

for our life there, thanks again!

心，血，心跳，心律失常，血壓和藥（國際英文版）
中風（癱瘓），骨頭，肩膀疼痛

Also to my dearest sons

*Noland and Alvin Cheung*

張俊璞, 張俊文

*Heart, Blood, Heartbeat, Arrhythmia, Blood Pressure & Drug Stroke (suffer paralysis), Bone, Shoulder Damaged*

# Preface

## In our Body

Sooner or later, our body feel not well. We will get sick. For this reason, we need to get doctor to treat his comfortable. Then doctor needs to get medicine for his treatment. After treatment we feel ok no problem anymore. Medicine is also always there in our body.

However, we should need to get medicine for the treatment. Truly, it needs medicine for treatment. It is a good idea for us to treat it.

But medicine is good for us them. However, it is not true. Medicine it also hurt his body later. Because medicine used often to hurt his body. It gets medicine amount more from each time in used. Sooner or later, it will get over dose amount later there. The over dose will have problem in our body later. We will find, it is not comfortable there in our later age. Definitely we will have all kind problem and disease there. It is such as hypertension happened and others there.

From this point, we have problem. It is due to medicine amount too much in our body there. Medicine amount used is the one to this problem on human

*Cheung Hong Son*

Warrenale, Pittsburgh, Pennsylvania USA

*February 8, 2020*

*Heart, Blood, Heartbeat, Arrhythmia, Blood Pressure & Drug*
*Stroke (suffer paralysis), Bone, Shoulder Damaged*

# Acknowledgement

I would like to thank those who supported me in writing this book.

In alphabetical order, they were Alvin Cheung, Noland Cheung, Sunhoo foo and Lisa Cheung.

I also would like to thank those who revised this book or other issues with all kind of suggestions. They were Alvin Cheung and Noland Cheung

心，血，心跳，心律失常，血壓和藥（國際英文版）
中風（癱瘓），骨頭，肩膀疼痛

# Chapter 1

## Pressure in our human body

Genetic surely, it born everything in our body there.

In human body, they must have water and blood together, but without water, they can't get blood in body there. Without water and blood there we can't get survival there.

For this reason, surely, we must get water and blood together in our body.

Energy relates with present in our body there to stay there. From there we will have everything there in our body. Water and blood are also there.

Pressure is there. High pressure could be happened there. High pressure present in our body, we must have medicine to get the pressure in lower situation there. Medicine is required. One of them, it needs such as beta blocker medicine present there. Medicine, present will block (release) the pressure high situation in our body. Medicine must be there. This kind medicine presents to make the pressure lower there and gone. Therefore, this medicine is required to this material must be there.

Pressure is here, certainly medicine must be there also as blood present in human body.

In blood, such material must be present in the normal pressure situation. But naturally material, it used there, later it used and gone not anymore. Therefore, the pressure high situation will be not happened there. No such naturally material is there. We must use from pharmaceutically company to make medicine there (such as using beta blocker, Capoten). Without the naturally material present there, pressure will be higher there. It is dangerous in our body to use.

*High pressure must be not there.*

# Chapter 2

## Heart *** Blood

Heartbeat (心跳, Heartbeat) is happened at all the time in our body and never stopped in our life until we end. Therefore, heartbeat is a very important in our life. Heartbeat if it is stopped. we died. Therefore, blood is always there. Life is there. It is there with blood together in our life. Therefore, blood in our body is very important to our body. Blood move in our body should be normally. In case blood moved is not ok as normal. We will have problem in our body and should feeling also bad. In case the blood is irregular moving, we feel bad and it also knowing when it happened to us.

Suppose, blood moved around irregular in flowing. Possibly you feel a dizzy situation in body, Blood amount is not enough there. It is dangerous.

心，血，心跳，心律失常，血壓和藥（國際英文版）
中風（癱瘓），骨頭，肩膀疼痛

Irregular situation causes blood missing, air and oxygen missing there too. Arrhythmia happened will be hurt in dangerous in our body.

*Heartbeat there.*

# Chapter 3

## Flexible situation *** blood moving

When age younger stronger, blood can be moved as normally no problem. When getting older, middle age (40 years older), person's blood does not that soften as flexible situation in blood. Blood moving will get irregular happened. The arrhythmia situation should have happened later. Therefore, it becomes the dangerous later to us. Arrhythmia situation surely is happened there and also not known to understand why happened "arrhythmia" situation here. Truly that situation is happened from the overdose happened there. It is this reason to get to know it. Thus, we should solve this problem from our understand in later to know what caused. It will explain later in our book there.

*Blood Flexible*

心，血，心跳，心律失常，血壓和藥（國際英文版）
中風（癱瘓），骨頭，肩膀疼痛

# Chapter 4

## Arrhythmia

Why is blood situation happened not normal there? Arrhythmia happened is there. Is it such as dizzy situation, oxygen not enough, energy missing, no force in body?

The blood situation must be not that normally there. Its blood situation is happened more or less in irregulate. Feeling it is not stable there, it is terrible.

Medicine amount could be used overdose there. This problem is not what understand happened from our feeling. In blood situation, it possible to make blood moving and flowing less there and not normally. Even the situation it knows the blood feeling in our body. Therefore, blood moving can be irregular happened there. Theoretically it will cause blood more to irregular situation with blood present there. After this irregular happened, arrhythmia is there. It is really to understand hard for medicine to cause there.

How can it make understand the arrhythmia(心律失常) situation gone and not happened there? For this situation, it solves this problem, it should explain later. After I should to learn for that. It can explain it later by me.

Later it can explain, how arrhythmia situation can solve it. It is from previous chapter to explained to solve arrhythmia understand for this disease.

Arrhythmia is a medical term for an irregular heartbeat pattern. A person might miss some heartbeats or have more or less than to the normal heartbeats there. The fact someone has arrhythmia there. It should have heart problem. Even found some people from time to time often with healthy hearts experience there, but their irregular pattern found there still often. They might not be aware what happening. Therefore, this situation It is not clear to know why. They have no symptoms there. Sometimes a doctor discovers this problem during a standard medical checkup. Heart disease can be a serious blood there for suffering. But no blood clear disease found for this situation. Otherwise it is healthy there. Problem it cannot be solved and explained later.

Usually patient and disease want to take for drug treated it. For the doctor treats the arrhythmia, why situation happened not normal there? Arrhythmia happened is there. Is it such as dizzy situation, oxygen not enough, energy missing, no force in body?

The blood situation must be not that normally there. Its blood situation is happened more or less in irregulate. Feeling it is not stable there, it is terrible.

*Arrhythmia happened believable*

心，血，心跳，心律失常，血壓和藥（國際英文版）
中風（癱瘓），骨頭，肩膀疼痛

# Chapter 5

## Drug Talk

Drug usually is making by pharmaceutically company. It is using by 8 hours, 16 hours and 24 hours period there. They are a good idea to have those amounts there. Drug is a good idea to have stay longer as possible. It also a good idea to have more effective drug and better there too.

Theoretically it is good to have patient and doctor agreed to have longer period and better effective medicine there. Unfortunately found, it is not true. Longer period and better effective medicine were not a better for patients using it. From experiment study there, it is not true. From longer and effective one, it will explain later here.

I tried about 7 years more, and watching here daily with pressure values studies there. It found

心，血，心跳，心律失常，血壓和藥（國際英文版）
中風（癱瘓），骨頭，肩膀疼痛

with medicine used 3 times (morning, lunch and night, every day) with reading and checking there. After that, I got the true information, but it found different results from my understanding to study there. I also find another 40 years for understanding. Their situation of my blood, its irregular happened from arrhythmia happened there. it is bad and dangerous feeling in my life. It likes as dizzy faint happened, oxygen may not enough and air missed there. It is terrible here. I will explain it later to understanding it.

*Overdose happened.*

# Chapter 6

## Blood pressure

I used 40 years with pressure there. The medicine found it is also with normal pressure there. For this reason, medicine amount found there, pressure is ok no problem. Its pressure is about as normal value for 120 to 130 there. For this reason, pressure value is ok. I used that pressure every day ok. Later I found that pressure, it is not working anymore. Pressure value is higher and pressure can't control anymore from there.

Therefore, doctor must change medicine to solve this problem. It must change the different medicine to get it working again. After again it works. After many years later, it is not working again. They need changing different medicine again to get working again. After it changed, the medicine, pressure is backing again to normal.

Why the working is happened again? Doctor is not surely why happened. It is also not understand happened, why is it get back again. We tried to understand and why how to explained that later.

From now, this time, I found the pressure value is little low, but its systolic is 55 to 62 value. However, the feeling found is not that well, but pressure reading is still ok. Then after 3 to 4 months later. I went to ask doctor to get changing the medicine to use dose again.

Medicine is hypertension (Beta blocker, Metoprolol) there using. I tried to use computer there. It used to measure the blood value there. It calculates the pressure value and it also save value it. Therefore, I have all results for me. The result is in my file and in my computer to save it.

Because I have results in computes. Later I ask the doctor to change medicine amount to 25 mg, 12 hours for 2 times a day. I used that daily. Once in the early morning, the other is in evening. From morning pressure value is ok. But in the later evening, the pressure is high. This situation is in every day.

For this reason, I talk to the doctor and change dose situation again to 12.5 mg each time, but now it is changed to 3 times using a day.

I try it, after a year, I found the pressure is ok every day. After a one year later, my pressure value is constant ok normal (12.5 mg).

Unbelieve my blood situation, found, that the irregular (Arrhythmia) situation changes to the stable situation there. This is the unbelievable situation happened. The arrhythmia is gone and no trouble any more. It is from very low dose situation caused.

Why arrhythmia situation is not anymore? Why happened arrhythmia is gone and back to the normal? Because it is, the amount of overdose is not there anymore, arrhythmia is also gone. From those results, you get there. High pressure situation is gone. It is also because of no overdose situation there, it means pressure is gone. No overdose is also gone too. They relate to each other. It is because of overdose there, it also means medicine amount is too high, overdose, pressure to this problem happened. The amount is too much to cause problem in our human in body there. Amount overdose is the true problem at all there.

心，血，心跳，心律失常，血壓和藥（國際英文版）
中風（癱瘓），骨頭，肩膀疼痛

Pressure is gone, high pressure is not there. Arrhythmia also missed, Again It means, overdose amount there, it truly is caused to our body.

They both is gone in our body. High pressure is the only problem to us.

*Heart, Blood, Heartbeat, Arrhythmia, Blood Pressure & Drug Stroke (suffer paralysis), Bone, Shoulder Damaged*

# Chapter 7

## Medicine

The question is for the blood of medicine mentioned here. We use medicine in our body and is also for doctor using it. Dr changes the amount for medicine to used several times.

Medicine using 8 hour, 16 and 24 hours are a day. It also likes to get more effective pill there.

For this amount it used 8 hours situation there, after that. The medicine needs to get a pill there. After that we continue to supply to use it, the amount of medicine after used it is until used. It continues to use it. It never stops. Only the fresh pill is there. For this situation, it is no left again, Theory, fresh pill used, it used and gone. For this reason, over dose could not be happened there anymore.

As this situation, the over dose situation is not happened any more. Using this way, over dose situation is never happened again.

Later I didn't use this situation but also not use doctor's idea. I try to my own way.

Following, I found the better way. I want to change a different medicine this time. It using 12.5 mg beta blocker, it is 8 hours each time, 3 times a day. This way, it is a very low dose pill for patient used. Therefore, dose amount is very low dose used. We must use this pill this way. Pill period is not last longer for stayed there. Almost all medicine is used and it is not using any more. After that, it is gone, following this situation, it is with fresh pill immediately again there. Overdose amount is never happened again. Fresh pill is always there. This situation can solve this problem for our body and no overdose happened. Pressure is not happened. Using this way try it, I never get pressure to high again.

Blood pressure is ok to me. Therefore, medicine here used no problem.

It needs new medicine to use and also with fresh pill there. After that from them, over dose amount will not be happened in our body from now on. Following we should have all problems missing there. The unbelief situation of arrhythmia is also gone and not in our body anymore.

But following the two years later from studied of blood pressure measuring, every day to me here. The low dose amount of pressure and blood flowing is gone, arrhythmia situation is not happened anymore.

Arrhythmia, the original normal situation is back to there.

For low dose pill uses it. The fresh pill is continued to use medicine there. The high dose medicine is not used anymore. They found this low dose amount is working well. Also, it found that blood pressure is evenly happened there. This is the reason to know, that high pressure is not happened any more. Arrhythmia is also not happened.

Blood pressure amount surely should be not high any more. It means, the medicine of amount is using low dose. Its pressure is ok there.

Therefore, pressure is ok, its Blood flowing, pressure in our body is normal. The blood present is ok in our body. Arrhythmia is also back normal. It means Low dose medicine, Pressure back normal, blood flowing ok, Arrhythmia back normal. Therefore, low dose medicine happened there, it caused everything happened normally in our body. It is very important to know that.

Therefore, when we get older, the natural blood medicine material is loss more and missing in our body. We must need to get the medicine for pressure to help our body. But naturally medicine material is loss. We need to get this artificial material to help.

For this reason, when we get older, we should get artificial medicine (as natural beta blocker) to get help. Theoretically they need this kind natural blood pressure medicines there. But truly It is not that way.

Young person, you already have nature medicine there in your body to provide. Old and older person, sooner or later nature high pressure of medicine dose is missing more in the pressure there. We need to get this missing medicine there. Otherwise we will have the problem here.

Medicine even it is missing later. We still need to get this kind natural medicine there.

The artificial medicine must supply it. After we get this artificial medicine. Then we will get the blood pressure back again. It likes to get the medicine (as beta blocker and others) to have it. Others our blood medicine is missing there. It must be to have here.

How can it solve this problem?

My blood pressure values measuring found is not that evenly there. The results they found high there. Doctor cannot control pressure well. For this situation, I leave that way, it is already for 40 years there.

For this way I used medicine there for me already.

心，血，心跳，心律失常，血壓和藥（國際英文版）
中風（癱瘓），骨頭，肩膀疼痛

Later I stayed in the New Jersey there and also for 3 years. I used medicine amount there and with this amount of dose here.

The dose of the amount, it used Beta blocker 50 mg daily as used that times. Later I changed to 25 mg. I don't like that dose amount there. It changed medicine to the 3 times a day or also use 2 times a day.

It also changed the doctor to use with low dose amount of beta blocker 25 mg 2 times a day there.

Here, it is including with the above 3 years of New Jersey stayed medicine there. it changed the medicine to 12.5 mg 3 times a day.

It is low dose pill to use this time. Following the pill continue to use until finished to get another fresh one there, It is never stopped there to use. The dose amount is happened there all the time. Therefore, overdose situation is not happened.

It is ok daily using. For patient used, this low dose amount, it never gets overdose happened there. It is from this low dose. The over dose it is not the trouble happened in our body there. Therefore, the medicine amount (of high dose there) is the one to have the trouble in human

But medicine used here, it is using regular with normal amount patient. In case, pressure patient higher possible can't be controlled well. Unless you must change use different medicine to solve this problem. After changed, pressure is backed to normal. However, after that, for a quite while the pressure is not working any again. Unless you want to change to get new medicine there. This is happened again and not working again. Unless You want to change different pill again. This situation will be happened working continue there.

Unless You should use different method to work again Different method should be used as.

It talks mention about this before. We must use low dose amount in our body that is all. It uses low dose there this problem is gone.

Talking about the medicine again, Short term medicine can be used as medicine. Long term medicine also can be used as medicine too. Both of they should be as good medicine. However. Long term, medicine could be hold pill 24 hour longer using a day. Short term, cannot be use for 24 hours long a day. It uses for 8 hour or as 16 hours longer. For this situation the period of medicine can be used more often.

Long term can be hold longer and stayed longer and not changed that often in a day.

Its advanged, it makes medicine in more effective pill for using and not that often for doctor and patient used.

For dis advanged, certainly low dose is often happened to use. Medicine is hold not that longer to use.

Medicine is very low dose amount to use there. This low dose amount can be used and holder stayed for 8 hours. It is supposed until all amount finished to use. This pill amount should be holder for using in short term body. It is a good idea for not overdose human use it.

From before I talked the truly, it is become no overdose medicine there to use mentioned here. It is not used and stayed that often because medicine is only can be used for short period to use there. Long term situation can be stay and using long time for more effective as using for medicine. Both of them was found with the pressure happened there.

Blood pressure value found is high there. The doctor will treat for them. Medicine such as ACE inhibitor, beta blocker and others can be used to treat.

After treated, medicine may use it. It works ok, no problem there.

But later a quite while, the medicine found is not work well with there. Unless you must to take a different medicine to use it to make pressure back again. After that, pressure is not work again. It needs to get new pills back again. This is the only way to solve this problem. However, it is after back for a while. It could be not working again anymore.

You have to use different pill again. You have to change different Pill again.

Because of the medicine after used, it is still stayed there. Medicine is still remaining. you can get remaining more or more again. Therefore, over dose medicine could be happened there. Then medicine is with over dose more there. The fresh medicine also keeps in continue there. Over dose pill, of course is still happened there. Because over dose present, it makes pressure <u>not control</u> anymore. This is the reason used new pill to back again. It is happened from over dose situation caused.

This problem we found.

It can use low dose amount for solve this problem. But for this way, you no need to use different pill to use it again and again.

Unless no overdose used this method. No overdose method will be explained, why pressure is not working anymore.

Finally, medicine used, it is for patient and doctor treatment. It is truly for treatment. Medicine is a good for disease treatment. However, it found from experience after 5 years pressure values studies founding. It is not true. Because, medicine used it is also not true. Medicine used in our body so often later, overdose will get happened there. From this reason we should get low dose medicine here. Use low dose, pressure also gone not any more. This Medicine used will cause problem. Medicine is also caused arrhythmia found problem. Medicine of arrhythmia also cause both situations there. Same kind medicines but caused happened from different disease.

Theoretical, medicine is the true problem in our body using. Besides, medicine is the only one to give his trouble.

心，血，心跳，心律失常，血壓和藥（國際英文版）
中風（癱瘓），骨頭，肩膀疼痛

# Chapter 8

## Blood Pressure value results

1. Why is people to get high pressure happened there in human body?
2. Is human to get pressure higher there?

It is because of high pressure present there. Present is there, blood and water (liquid there) are together. Pressure is from energy there. Surely pressure is from high situation happened. This is the reason why to get high pressure to be there. Pressure there, we need pressure of medicine such as Capoten there to get lower of its blood pressure situation there. This medicine present is there, theoretically its high pressure is release to the lower situation.

Medicine use too often with longer period pill of 24 hours there. Sooner or later, many medicines left is remaining but still not finish there. Many pills remaining, those become more or more there. More left, the over dose amount will be happened. More left, it is side effect happened. High pressure medicine will not work anymore. For this reason, they must change different to use medicine to make it working again. This is the reason to make high pressure to back to the normal situation there.

It is over dose there. If we change to use medicine amount to low dose. Pressure situation will be better and better. Medicine can be as normally.

However, we tried to use the medicine amount, it is as following 12.5 mg, 3 times daily. It used medicine with very low dose amount. From 7 years studies with pressure values there, it shows long term studies here. It is about shows from the October 2019 to here. It shows only partially ok.

10/01/19  Tus  星期二  132/84/62  6/22 AM:

136/84/59 2/52 PM: 130/80/68  8/05 PM:  12.5 mg

10/02/19  Wed  星期三  138/81/64  5/37 AM:

134/81/75 0/52 PM: 131/83/69  6/12 PM: 12.5 mg

心，血，心跳，心律失常，血壓和藥（國際英文版）
中風（癱瘓），骨頭，肩膀疼痛

10/03/19 Thu　星期四　131/81/60　6/53 AM:

　　136/80/65　1/37 PM: 135/81/59　5/13 PM: 12.5 mg

10/04/19 Fri　星期五　131/81/65　6/05 AM:

　　134/81/62　11/42 AM: 128/73/65　9/51 PM: 12.5 mg

10/05/19 Sat　星期六　124/80/67　6/22 AM:

　　140/79/60　9/16 PM: 132/81/63　11/05 PM　12.5 mg

10/06/19 Sun　星期日　128/80/64　6/06 AM:

　　136/84/61　11/37 PM: 140/82/60　8/14 PM　12.5 mg

10/07/19 Mon　星期一　134/81/57　6/01 AM:

　　114 /72/63　0/28 PM: 137/76/56　9/02 PM　12.5 mg

10/08/19`Tus　星期二　133/83/58　5/48 AM:

　　128/75/70　1/05 PM:　137/84/76　6/03 PM: 12.5 mg

10/09/19 Wed　星期三　130/78/61　5/38 AM:

　　108/66/69　0/42 PM: 132/75/66　8/05 PM　12.5 mg

10/10/19 Thu　星期四　133/81/67　6/01 AM:

　　136/79/60 11/23 AM:

*Heart, Blood, Heartbeat, Arrhythmia, Blood Pressure & Drug*
*Stroke (suffer paralysis), Bone, Shoulder Damaged*

10/11/19  Fri  星期五  126/80/66  6/24 AM:

124/73/68 11/27 AM: 117/72/60  5/34  PM: 12.5 mg

10/12/19  Sat  星期六  107/80/93  5/32 AM:

128/79/77 2/32 PM: 127/76/77  8/24 PM: 12.5 mg

10/13/19  sun  星期日  128/79/64  6/08 AM:

130/75/6 11/43 AM: 126/77/63  9/14 PM: 12.5 mg

10/14/19  Mon  星期一  130/77/69  5/53 AM:

128/73/6 11/04 AM: 134/82/58  5/08 PM: 12.5 mg

10/15/19  Tus  星期二  127/80/60  5/26 AM:

133/83/65  0/39 PM:  12.5 mg

10/16/19  Wed  星期三  132/80/64  6/13 AM:

127/77/62 11/02 AM: 134/80/64  7/56 PM: 12.5 mg

10/17/19  Thu  星期四  130/77/73  8/38 AM:

142/84/67 7/56 PM:  130/84/72  9/07 PM: 12.5mg

10/18/19  Fri  星期五  134/85/71  6/01 AM:

130/72/74  1/51 PM: 130/72/64  10/07  PM:12.5 mg

心，血，心跳，心律失常，血壓和藥（國際英文版）
中風（癱瘓），骨頭，肩膀疼痛

10/19/19 Sat　　星期六　123/79/68　6/13 AM:

　　　　　128/81/63　11/02 PM　12.5 mg

10/20/19 Sun 星期日 121/79/70　5/37 AM:

　　112/72/74　00/01PM: 133/80/61　6/01 PM 12.5 mg

10/21/19 Mon　星期一 124/78/64 6/01 AM:

　　123/77/70　11/17AM: 118/70/67　7/29 PM　12.5 mg

10/22/19 Tus　　星期二 132/81/59 5/38 AM:

　　127/81/70　11/58 AM: 136/78/57　6/12 PM 12.5 mg

10/23/19 Wed　星期三 139/80/70　6/18 AM:

　　124/71/62 11/05 AM　12.5 mg


It is too long. I only get part of that results here.

　　　　　　　　　　Pressure value results here.

# Chapter 9

## My stroke Paralysis

Stroke (suffer paralysis) 中風,bone, shoulder, 肩膀

About 60 years age old person, his body is not that stronger. It also found it is not that support well too. I went to wax the car and fall down to the drive way. It is ok no problem this time.

Next time, I didn't supply the body well. Then I fall down to the drive way. My whole body his shoulder and bone fall down together and damaged. Lucky, it is not hurting that time. It is ok to me. This time, the stroke is not happened at all.

Third time (next years later) I waxed the same car and also fall down to this car. It is also hurt again with same place of same driveway and same shoulder and bone damaged again. It is not that lucky. But stroke is slight damaged. It is not well but sooner and later. It is back to the normal.

The fourth times, (another next years) I waxed the same car, also same drive way. I fall down to drive way and damaged to same shoulder and same bone. This time I hurt my body immediately, I lost my vision, I can't see it clean. This time It is terrible situation to me.

I know my feeling, it is not lucky again. My memory is terrible. I can't know whom there. I don't know understand at all.

Later, after that I have to learn little and little each time. It is such as to write 26 letters. Later write, (the words, time, minute, hours, day, numbers and following) also learns the computer with English also Chinese text and meaning there. From the first important things to back from stroke back. My sons (Noland and Alvin) tell me how to use work as mentioned there. After it knows the stroke person found easily forgot to lose memory there. Then I must to write those remember things to save it immediately in my computer to use it. I must save it again for stroke person to remine again. This is a very important to help for me.

*Heart, Blood, Heartbeat, Arrhythmia, Blood Pressure & Drug*
*Stroke (suffer paralysis), Bone, Shoulder Damaged*

From those help. I can understand what computer can writing to me. Thus stroke, it can talk to me. Computer is also talk to them.

Stroke to me.

心，血，心跳，心律失常，血壓和藥（國際英文版）
中風（癱瘓），骨頭，肩膀疼痛

# Chapter 10

## Xarelto pill and condition

After stroke happened to me, I must use this medicine for doctor treated. This medicine name is Xarelto (Bayer) Anticoagulant again.

I must use this medicine (Xarelto from Bayer) here.

It looks like anticoagulant and as blood likes. After years using, I found blood leaking out into with urea together. A lot of blood leak out to the blood into my body. Many amounts of blood lost into urea. It feels dizzy. It was dangerous to me.

Later, hospital give me serval times for blood bank to help.

It is blood losing there and leaking into the urea also to my body.

I asked doctor to stop this (Xarelto) to use this medicine (Xarelto) for me.

I have asked doctor, asking any doctor to use any medicine to take it over for not using Xarelto there. Best situation, that is still using Xarelto medicine here. I talk to every people, only doctor, Kudryk said yes. You can change to this way. It is not a medicine to use it.

It is different method. It is from the Iron shots (infusion) method here. Later, it sent the service to use iron infusion there. It worked for total six times, each with using 300 cc (liters) there. After that, Xarelto would be no longer use this medicine forever.

However, I found that the iron infusion service for me. It is correctly, But the amount possible could be too much used. Over dose could be happened there. I talked to the doctor for this. They didn't worry it.

After finished from the service, later, blood happened again with urine as before. Blood there, the dangerous situation also happened to me again.

However, over dose of iron shot caused more blood there. This over dose made the blood there, it also caused over dose to block blood precipitate there.

After that, no Xarelto used in this medicine forever.

However, I found that the iron infusion service for me. The amount would be possible too much. Over dose could be happened to there. I talked to the doctor for this. They didn't worry it.

After finished from the service, later, blood happened again with urine as before. This precipitate here is terrible in my body. Precipitation is still there.

However, iron shot caused from over dose is still in blood there together. The precipitation of blood blocked is there. Therefore, the blood was still in the urine there. Blood is never stopping the blood there. I wondered why blood in the urines never stopped. It looked liking no ending for blood stopping in urine there. Noland and Alvin asked that iron infusion still there and must ending where.

For this reason, doctor helps me to try stop the blood there. They try to use with water filled solution into my blood line. It used many bottles and liquids from the day and night to continued. It is never stopped. It changed water and liquids there. It takes many bottles, liquids and water there to work and services together. It used about 15 days to work continuing.

心，血，心跳，心律失常，血壓和藥（國際英文版）
中風（癱瘓），骨頭，肩膀疼痛

Precipitation is removed away. Finally, blood is gone and as clear bloodless, as water solution.

This doctor works so hard. Finally, he couldn't find any blood there in urine. It also should be no blood as bloodless in the blood solution in my body and urine there. No blood finds there.

Now, iron infusion is not found in my body anymore. Instead it changed back to the true nature blood in my body there.

From now on, I use the true nature blood again in my life. I didn't have worry about any blood situation there. Xarelto is no blood anymore for using in my body. I feel ok again for me.

Xarelto trouble there.

*Heart, Blood, Heartbeat, Arrhythmia, Blood Pressure & Drug*
*Stroke (suffer paralysis), Bone, Shoulder Damaged*

# Conclusion

**The reason for publishing this book is because**

**I got stroke (中風)**

It is so hard to write this book for stroke person like me.

I have to write about this book. It can help this health for human body.

**Truly medicine is good, but used in problem with overdose using in our body later**

心，血，心跳，心律失常，血壓和藥（國際英文版）
中風（癱瘓），骨頭，肩膀疼痛

# Heart, Blood, Heartbeat, Arrhythmia, Blood Pressure & Drug

Stroke (suffer paralysis), Bone, Shoulder Damaged

## 心，血，心跳，心律失常，血壓和藥
中風（癱瘓），骨頭，肩膀疼痛（國際英文版）

Author / Hong Son Cheung
*https://www.amazon.com/author/hongson.cheung*

Publisher / EHGBooks United States
http://www.TaiwanFellowship.org
Date / April 2020
Distribution Channels
**Online**
    Amazon.com
**China**
    Xiamen International Book Company Limited
    Add: 4 / F, Logistics Building, No.8, Yuehua Road,
    Huli District, Xiamen City China
    Direct Line / 0592-5061658、6028707
**Taiwan**
    Sanmin Bookstores / http://www.sanmin.com.tw
    Add: No. 386, Fuxing N. Road, Taipei Taiwan
    Add: No. 61, Chongqing S. Road, Taipei Taiwan
    Direct Line / 02-2500-6600、02-2361-7511
    Kingstone Bookstores / http://www.kingstone.com.tw

Price / US$15 / NT$450 / RMB$100

*2020 © United States, Permission required for reproduction, or translation in whole or part.*

www.ingramcontent.com/pod-product-compliance
Lightning Source LLC
LaVergne TN
LVHW091934070526
838200LV00068B/1195